The Hiawatha Trail
An Allegory

Philip M. Hudson

Copyright 2020 by Philip M. Hudson.

Published 2020.

Printed in the United States of America.

All rights reserved.

No portion of this book may be reproduced, stored in a retrieval system, or transmitted in any form or by any means - electronic, mechanical, photocopy, recording, scanning, or other - except for brief quotations in critical reviews or articles, without the prior written permission of the author.

ISBN 978-1-950647-54-5

Illustrations - Google Images.

This book may be ordered from online bookstores.

Publishing Services by BookCrafters
Parker, Colorado.
www.bookcrafters.net

Table of Contents

Foreword..i
Prologue..vii
The Hiawatha Trail: An Allegory...1

Author's Note...95
Afterword..109
About The Author...125
By The Author..127

Foreword

Adversity
can be the star
dust that polishes
us to a high luster,
but it can also be an
abrasive that wears us
down and grinds us
up. It all depends
upon how we
use it.

In this allegory,
Haidyn Hudson serves
as a role model for those
who would embrace adversity
as a God-given opportunity
for personal growth and
achievement.

Prologue

Spencer W. Kimball taught that it seems to be our nature to try to "expel from our lives physical pain and mental anguish and to assure ourselves of continual ease and comfort, but if we were to close the doors upon such sorrow and distress, we might be excluding our greatest friends and benefactors. Suffering can make saints of people as they learn patience, long-suffering, and self-mastery."

x

"If all the sick for whom we pray were healed, if all the righteous were protected and the wicked destroyed, the whole program of the Father would be annulled. The basic principle of the gospel would be ended, for no-one would have to live by faith. If joy and peace and rewards were instantaneously given the doer of good, there could be no evil – all would do good and not because of the rightness of doing good. There would be no test of strength, no development of character, no growth of powers, no (agency, but) only satanic controls."

Oh, the wisdom of Father Lehi,
when he declared: "It must need be that
there is opposition in all things!" (2 Nephi 2:11).
Thanks be to our Father in Heaven and to Adam
and Eve for making it possible to have posterity
in mortality's stimulating environment. For
our benefit, we become acquainted with
darkness as well as with light, with
pleasure as well as with pain,
and with sorrow as well
as with happiness.

God's great Plan of Deliverance from Death was carefully crafted to create the conditions to come unto Christ within the crucible of mortal experience. Perhaps there is sense, after all, in the seeming chaos of existence, and there is a common thread underlying all experience. "For my thoughts are not your thoughts, neither are your ways my ways, saith the Lord. For as the heavens are higher than the earth, so are my ways higher than your ways, and my thoughts than your thoughts."
(Isaiah 55:8-9).

The Hiawatha Trail

"I shall be telling this with a sigh somewhere ages and ages hence: Two roads diverged in a wood, and I, I took the one less traveled by, and that has made all the difference."
(Robert Frost).

An allegory for our time

In 2016, I had the opportunity to ride my bicycle along the Hiawatha Trail with my nine-year-old granddaughter, Haidyn. The route of the Hiawatha mountain biking and hiking trail winds its way for 15 miles through the Bitterroot Mountains of North Idaho and Western Montana, while traversing 10 train tunnels and negotiating 7 sky-high trestles. Still called the Milwaukee Road, when it was completed over a century ago, it became one of the most scenic stretches of railroad in the country. The "Route of the Hiawatha" is most famous for the Taft Tunnel, which burrows for 8,771 ft. (1.66 miles) under the Bitterroots at the state line.

Switch points in our lives

As we started our bike ride, the thought struck me that Haidyn had reached the age of accountability and now found herself in the valley of decision. As we started the journey from the parking lot and entered the first tunnel, I thought about the physical, emotional, and even the doctrinal switch points that she would face along the ride.

Of all things, I thought about NASAs moon missions, each of which was ultimately dependent upon a precise trajectory that would bring the command module back to earth. To accomplish that, during the 240,000-mile passage from the moon, a number of course corrections had to be made, utilizing rocket "burns" of precise duration. Upon reaching the earth's atmosphere, the entry window was less than 2 degrees. If the earth were a basketball, and the space capsule a grain of sand, it would have to enter the atmosphere at a trajectory with a margin of error no wider than a piece of paper. Otherwise it would either come in at too steep an angle and burn up, or it would come in too shallow, skip off the atmosphere and bounce back into space and away from the earth. There would be no second chance for Mission Control back in Houston to make a good first impression.

Challenging terrain

Although the terrain at the crest of the Bitterroot Mountains appeared challenging, the consequences of poor decision-making on Haydyn's part were not as significant as that of lunar astronauts. Still, with every pedal stroke, the necessity of successfully completing the 15 miles of the Milwaukee Road increased. For a terrestrial explorer suited up in a nine-year old's body, it would be a daunting task, even though the constant downgrade of 1.25% would ameliorate her physical stress.

Haidyn had barely started on the trail, when she encountered her first obstacle, the Taft Tunnel that burrowed beneath the crest of the Bitterroots. Negotiating the tunnel would take her from her Montana starting point westward into Idaho. Two hundred yards in, the light from the entrance was smothered by a blackness that was the equivalent of pitch slowly oozing over the eyes. Even the water dripping from the rock walls and ceiling was black. It had the certain texture of a vaguely wet aether, but it was without form or substance. All Haidyn could do was keep her eyes fixed on the light from the headlamps of cyclists ahead of her and keep pedaling steadily forward. The beam from her own headlamp only faintly illuminated the walls of the tunnel, and as I strained to see her, she seemed to be standing still, while it was the silent rock that slipped by like a ghost ship in the night.

Riding into darkness

The darkness seemed to suck the air from our lungs, and with our eyes we were unable to focus on the encroaching walls of granite. They seemed about to reach out and snag us. As Haidyn resolutely pedaled on, I thought of a recollection of Boyd K. Packer. He said: "Shortly after I was called as a General Authority, I went to Elder Harold B. Lee for counsel. He listened very carefully to my problem and suggested that I see President David O. McKay, who then counseled me as to the direction I should go. I was very willing to be obedient, but saw no way possible for me to do as he said.

I returned to Elder Lee and told him that I saw no way to move in the suggested direction. He said: 'The trouble with you is you want to see the end from the beginning.' I replied that I would like to see at least a step or two ahead. Then came the lesson of a lifetime: 'You must learn to walk to the edge of the light, and then a few steps into the darkness. Then, the light will appear and show the way before you.' Then, he quoted scripture: 'Dispute not because ye see not, for ye receive no witness until after the trial of your faith.' (Ether 12:6)." ("BYU Magazine," 3/1991).

A spiritual
strong searchlight

Haidyn had a long 15 minutes inside the Taft Tunnel to put into practice that wise counsel. She was doing so well that, at one point, she called out to her dad, who was riding nearby, and actually asked if she could turn off her light. I am not sure why she did that, but it may have been because she wanted to savor the raw, untinctured experience of walking (or pedaling) by faith. Perhaps she wanted to focus on the uncommon opportunity to literally wrap all of her physical senses around adversity and call upon her spiritual reserves to carry the day. She may have intuitively realized that she was being given a unique chance to increase her confidence, to control and master her emotions, and to confront and overcome her fears. She may have known that the experience would provide unprecedented preparation for her encounter with the next inevitable tunnel on her journey through life, providing her with invaluable experience so that it would not catch her off-guard.

Seeing with the eye of faith

When Haidyn was a few hundred yards from the end of the Taft Tunnel, she could begin to vaguely see what at first appeared to be only a tiny pinpoint of light. But as she pedaled on, that faint glow grew larger and larger until it assumed the shape of an exit. In the gathering light, she began to be able to make out features within the tunnel itself, and to see the pedals, handlebars, and handgrips of her bicycle. She could see her hands and her feet, as well as the forms of those who had been steadily cycling nearby, but who, until this moment, had been within the veil of darkness, and invisible to her eyes.

Heavenly Father
will never leave us

Haidyn knew that her companions had been there all along, because from time to time they had called out words of encouragement to her. Had it not been so dark, the frost on their breath would have betrayed the temperature inside the tunnel, which was 40 degrees colder than the ambient air temperature on the trail. Haidyn had taken fresh courage each time she had heard those familiar voices, but now, as she moved into the light, she was infused with an overwhelming sense of courage that replaced her hesitancy and dissipated her fears. She was thrilled to feel them evaporate with her return to the heat of the day.

Fresh courage take

As her eyes re-adjusted to the brilliant sunlight, Haidyn was quick to notice that she could little afford even a moment's distraction from the task that now lay before her with crystal clarity. For as far as she could see on the trail that stretched off into the distance, there were rocks on the path, and she soberly realized that they would, without relief, present challenges to her cycling skills. It was little consolation to her that many boulders had been previously cleared, because they were the ones that would have been easier to see in the first place. She would have had little difficulty avoiding them. It was the little rocks of irregular shape and size, and the gravel surface of the roadbed itself, that would prove to be most hazardous, should her concentration falter.

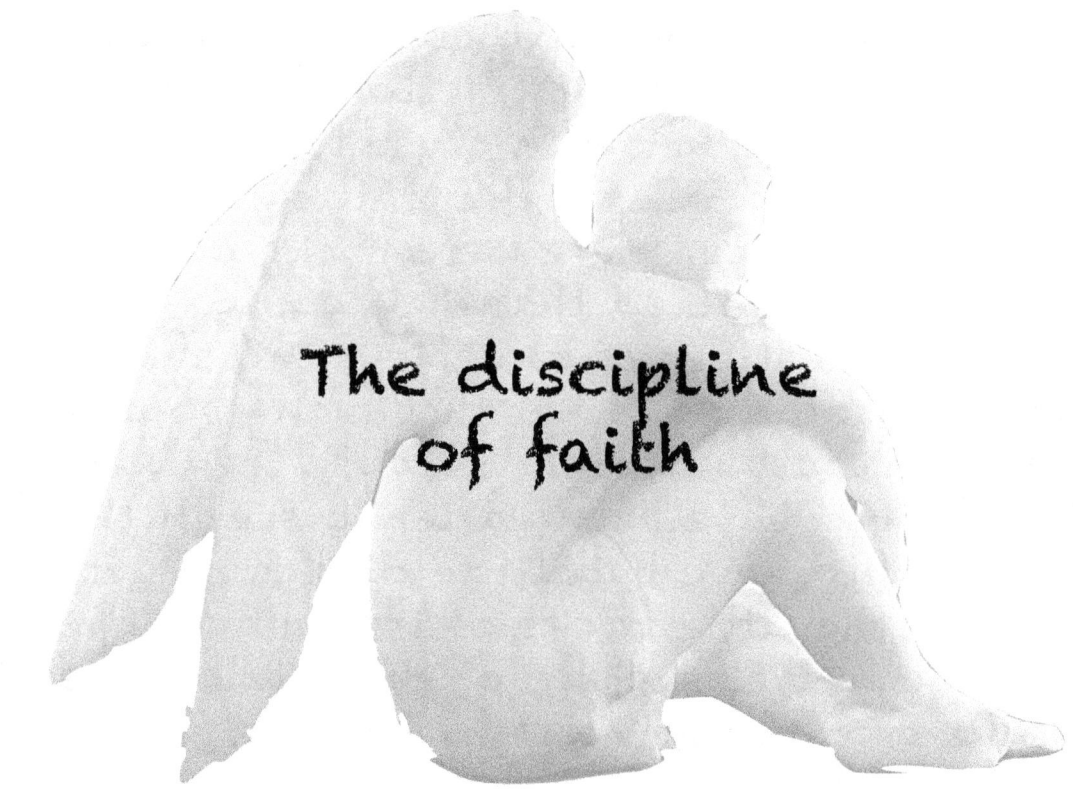
The discipline of faith

It became clear to Haidyn that she would need to move forward purposefully and steadily, in order to maintain her momentum and stability. She could not allow herself to weave back and forth across the straight and narrow path that lay before her. To do so would be to invite disaster. In fact, from time to time, as she adjusted to the conditions of the trail and eased up on her cadence, she could feel her front wheel washing out on the gravel. At these moments, the impending peril jerked her attention back to the road.

All these things
shall give thee
experience

She quickly learned to roll with these obstacles, and to her delight, found that, with practice, they would take care of themselves without her conscious attention. She realized, however, that if she braked too hard, her rear wheel would lock up and she would lose maneuverability. So, instead of quickening her pace and risking blowing a corner, she maintained steady forward momentum to maximize her progress and minimize risk.
She learned that if she were over-zealous, if she pedaled too fast, turned too sharply, or made major adjustments too quickly, she would find herself in trouble, without any viable options to re-establish control.

Opposition
in all things

That is not to say that Haidyn was able to eliminate opposition as she made her way along the 15 miles of the trail. The trip may have only taken 2 or 3 hours, but to her it felt like a lifetime. She put to use the skills she had learned while snow-skiing, and remembered that when she had been gliding smoothly and effortlessly along a run, she had been going downhill. The Hiawatha Trail was an unforgiving teacher, but Haidyn was a quick study who discovered that her best strategy would be to control her cadence and her breathing, and to push evenly against the pedals no matter that the resistance of the terrain might vary, or that the next rest stop might still be long minutes away.

Pain falls
drop by drop,
upon the heart

She had only one crash, but it hurt a lot. It happened so fast that she barely had time to react before her hand, forearm, and hip skidded along the ground. As I picked her up and held her closely, I thought about the fallen giants of the forest whose rings we have all traced with our fingers. We notice that the spacing between them is irregular, because the years of greatest growth are represented by the widest rings, reflecting years of abundant moisture from rain, much like Haidyn's tears.

Blindsided by life

Yes, tears were shed, but bravely she got back on the bike. I knew that Haidyn would be wiser for the experience and would be better prepared down the trail to avoid another close encounter of the dirt kind. I hoped she would be able to take away something positive from the crash. Maybe dumping her bike would give her a chance to reflect on the fact that we can be zooming along, standing on our pedals without a care in the world, with the wind in our faces and enjoying the freedom of the trail. Then, almost without warning, we might hit an obstacle that jerks our handlebars sideways and causes us to lose our sure grip and throw our inertia out of balance. Sometimes when we least expect it, we suddenly find ourselves in the dirt, one with mother earth, in a terrestrial reality-check that on closer inspection is one of God's tender mercies.

The real tragedy
is to have sight,
but no vision

How Haidyn handled that crash was similar to how she dealt with nine more tunnels that we encountered during our ride. Some, like the Taft Tunnel, were so long you couldn't see the end from the beginning. Others had enough of a curve to them that, even though they were not very long, the light at the end would be hidden from view as we started out. In any event, the darkness in many of them seemed to compress our chests and make breathing more labored. The sensory deprivation was "un-nerving" but it actually made us more acutely aware of our internal defense mechanisms designed to combat and triumph over unavoidable stress. I hoped that Haidyn would realize that in some of the tunnels that we encounter in life, the Sprit may seem to abandon us. We may have to suck it up when we feel that we have been forsaken.

In the case of the Taft Tunnel, which was the longest and hardest one to be negotiated, it had to be tackled from both directions, at the beginning and then again at the very end of the ride, inasmuch as the return shuttle bus dropped us off at the outbound exit. The greatest trials, it seems, are sometimes saved for last.

Stumbling blocks or stepping stones

A word about the seven trestles. They were hundreds of feet high, soaring above the valley floor. As intimidating as they may have initially seemed, it was clear that the trestles were our "friends" that had been provided by the engineers who constructed the road, in order to avoid thousands of feet of vertical loss and gain, in the negotiation of an intimidating chasm. The thought came to my mind as we approached the first trestle that the thoughtfulness of the railroad's civil engineers had been to put it within our power to soar as eagles rather than walk as turkeys, and to choose to fly.

Soar with eagles
or walk with turkeys

I thought of the words of the inspiring poem, that reads: "Oh, I have slipped the surly bonds of earth and danced the skies on laughter-silvered wings. Sunward I've climbed, and joined the tumbling mirth of sun-split clouds, and wheeled and soared and swung high in the sunlit silence. Hovering there, I've chased the shouting wind through footless halls of air. Up, up the long, delirious, burning blue I've topped the windswept heights with easy grace, where never lark, or even eagle flew. With silent lifting mind, I've trod the high untrespassed sanctity of space, put out my hand, and touched the face of God." (John Magee, "High Flight"). On those trestles, it seemed like we didn't need an aircraft to experience high flight. I quietly prayed that the joy of the moment would not be lost on Haidyn.

Hold on to the Rod of Iron

I pointed out to her that as we negotiate the trestles that have been constructed by God, and make our way along the strait and narrow path, high above the chasms that we encounter in life, we are protected on both the right and the left by an iron rod of security. In the case of the Hiawatha Trail, these were taut steel cables strategically stretched at heights of 6 inches, 12 inches, 18 inches, and so on, up to 4 feet high, to protect us from harm. The only way we could put ourselves in jeopardy of serious injury or death would have been if we were to have made a conscious and deliberate decision to disregard the safety mechanisms that had been provided by those who had carefully planned out the Route of the Hiawatha. As we negotiate the trestles of life, angels are silently taking notes, consulting with the Holy Ghost, and relying upon the Plan, to provide us with proven success strategies.

Endure to the end

There did come a point when Haidyn asked: "How much further do we have to go?" To her credit, there was no hint of complaint in her innocent inquiry. I think she only wanted some perspective. She was beginning to feel that she was approaching the limits of her endurance, never before having pedaled so far. She may have never been so tired, so hungry, or so thirsty. She wanted to finish what she had set out to do, but she realized that she had finite physical resources to accomplish the task at hand. It was at this point that she and I began to have a serious conversation about the emotional and spiritual reserves upon which she could draw in this time of real need. We talked about the relationships between ability, inability, and availability, between perspiration and inspiration, and about the fact that the dictionary is the only place where success comes before work. We discussed what it means to go the second mile.

Altitude is
all about attitude

We talked about the qualities of high-achievers, those who dream big, who have developed spirituality and are persons of known character, who have clearly defined and realistic goals, who do not procrastinate but accept responsibility, who establish priorities and stick with them, who consciously choose which habits will unconsciously govern much of their lives, who have single-minded concentration, who never consider the possibility of failure, who recognize and act upon the switch-points in their lives, who seize the moment, and who persist until they succeed.

Success strategies

As Haidyn doggedly pedaled on, had she seen a turtle on a fence post, she would have known one thing for certain: he had help getting up there. As a high-achiever, she would draw upon her experience to influence outcomes. She would know that if you put roller skates on an octopus, you won't necessarily know where it will go, but you will be sure that it will be a wild ride. As I watched Haidyn, I thought of these lines of prose: "The stars fade away, the sun himself grow dim with age, and nature sink in years. (But she) shall flourish in immortal youth, unhurt amidst the war of elements, the wreck of matter, and the crash of worlds." (Joseph Addison, "Cato" Act 5, Scene 1).

Free will

President Howard W. Hunter told the story of a summer day early in the morning, when he was standing near the window. "The curtains obstructed me," he said, "from two little creatures out on the lawn. One was a large bird and the other a little bird, obviously just out of the nest. I saw the larger bird hop out on the lawn, then thump his feet and cock his head. He drew a big fat worm out of the lawn and came hopping back. The little bird opened its bill wide, but the big bird swallowed the worm. There was squawking in protest. The big bird flew away, and I didn't see it again, but I watched the little bird. After a while, it hopped out on the lawn, thumped its feet, cocked its head, and pulled a big worm out of the lawn."

At one point, as Haidyn and I stopped for a nutrition break, I offered a silent prayer of gratitude that, as an eager participant in life, she was learning how to find "big fat worms."

Work out your salvation with fear and trembling

I briefly shared with her an experience I had as a young man. It had been my exercise habit to run 5 or 10 miles every morning, for an hour or two before sunrise. I ran through the Santa Monica Mountains, above our home in Pacific Palisades, in Southern California. One day, as I neared the end of my run, I regained the surface streets and began to trace my way back to my home. I stopped at an intersection, waiting for the traffic signal to change, and put my hands on my knees. With the sweat dripping off the end of my nose, I thought about throwing in the towel, stopping right then and there, and giving my complaining muscles a much-deserved rest. However, through sweat-soaked eyes, I looked up, and saw as it were, a vision before me. Insistently flashing red with neon brightness, directly in front of me, were two inspiring words that urged me on: "Don't walk!"

That message, as if from God Himself, prompted me to wonder: "What happens to us when we go the second mile?" As we learn to confront our trials and tribulations, by pushing just a little harder, we grow in the Spirit. It is no coincidence that the Savior linked two scriptures together: "Whosoever shall compel thee to go a mile, go with him twain," and then: "Be ye, therefore, perfect, even as your Father which is in heaven is perfect." (Matthew 5:38 & 48).

Our spiritual bank accounts

I hoped that as Haidyn approached the limits of her physical endurance, she would be pushing her emotional and spiritual boundaries, as well. I thought that as she discovered reserves of physical energy that she had not known she possessed, she would simultaneously be making deposits to her spiritual bank account, to be held in reserve for the moment when a desperate withdrawal might be required. I believed, and I think Haidyn might have also discovered, that pushing her physical boundaries would expand her spiritual capacity, and vice versa. Stretching would enlarge the circle of her experience and create new opportunities for growth.

Blood, sweat, toil, and tears

As Teddy Roosevelt famously observed: "It is not the critic who counts; not the one who points out how the strong stumble, or where the doer of deeds could have done them better. The credit belongs to the one who is actually in the arena, whose face is marred by dust and sweat and blood; who strives valiantly; who errs, who comes up short again and again, because there is no effort without error; but who actually strives to do the deeds; who knows great enthusiasms, the great devotions; who recognizes a worthy cause; who at the best knows in the end the triumph of high achievement, and who at the worst, at least fails while daring greatly, so that her place shall never be with those cold and timid souls who know neither victory nor defeat." ("Citizenship in a Republic," Speech at the Sorbonne, Paris, 4/23/1910).

Spiritually aerobic exercise

As we neared the end of the trail, I was confident that no matter how tired Haidyn felt, she would not experience defeat. She would triumph over every obstacle. In the future, she would be able to measure the difficulty of her challenges against her experience on the Hiawatha Trail. We talked about different scenarios. For example, in the future, as Haidyn faced new trials in the learning laboratory of life, she would be able to say: "If I can do that (the Route of the Hiawatha), I can do this!" Or: "I know that I can do this, because I did that (the Hiawatha)." In the future, because she had built new spiritual muscle, Haidyn would be better equipped to exercise her mortal frame.

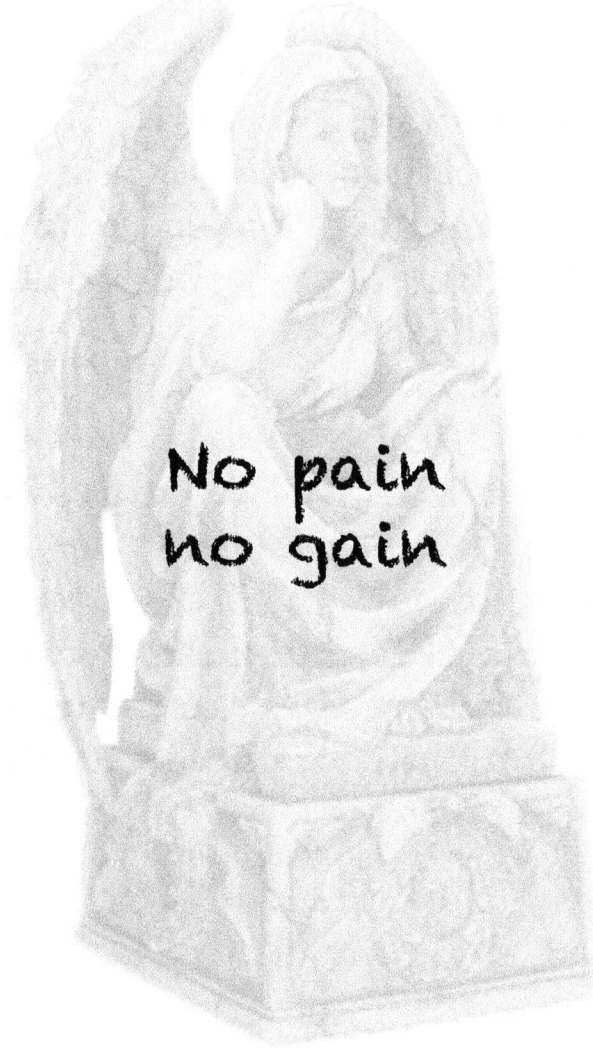

I warned her that she might be sore the day following such strenuous activity. But I also reminded her that perspiring every day is good therapy, and that breaking a soul-sweat is even better. If she could view her experiences on the Hiawatha Trail from a spiritual perspective, she would be doubly blessed. Spiritually aerobic exercise would be the best way to keep her physical body attuned to the Infinite. The process might initially take her breath away, but eventually it would endow her with an increased capacity to fill her lungs with celestial air, and it would introduce her to the refreshing breeze that cools the fires of the eternal world. It would allow her to feel the power of God.

The power of the Force

I told Haidyn that, as far as I was concerned, she had become a Jedi Knight, one who serves and utilizes that mystical power described as the Force to act in the capacity of a guardian of peace and justice in the galaxy. The philosophy of self-denial that is embraced by the Jedi stands in sharp contrast to that of their arch-enemies, the Sith, who usurp power to twist it to the dark side.

"May the Force be with you!" declared General Dodonna, before the Death Star battle in Episode 4 of the Star Wars saga. Obi-Wan Kenobe described the Force as "what gives a Jedi power. It's an energy field created by all living things. It surrounds us and penetrates us. It binds the galaxy together." On the Route of the Hiawatha, I could tell that the Force was strong with young Haidyn.

Beware
the Dark Side

I reminded her how the Master Teacher Yoda had explained to young Luke Skywalker: "A Jedi's strength flows from the Force. But beware of the dark side; anger, fear, aggression. The dark side are they. Easily they flow; quick to join you in a fight. If once you start down the dark path, forever will it dominate your destiny; consume you, it will." Part of Haidyn's Jedi training on the Hiawatha Trail would enhance her power to resist the temptation to yield to the power of the Sith.

A Divine Design

She was not alone on her journey, but was constantly shepherded by her parents and grandparents to keep her out of harms way, and they were pleased when she carefully listened to their counsel. They knew that she valued their experience, but they also realized that she still had to travel her own path, as she passed one milepost after another on her journey. No one else could do it for her. That was as it should have been, because God purposefully sets the bar high in order to establish a level of personal commitment that will help His children to see beyond limited horizons and remove the veil of insensitivity to their divine destiny.

Recognizing our Redeemer

We were close to the end of the ride when, to my great surprise, Haidyn asked: "When we get there, do we have to go back up again?" I thought: "Bless her heart!" She didn't ask in complaint, so that she might whine about the possibility. She just wanted to know. I reassured her that there would be a bus waiting for us, that would take us the 15 miles back to our car up at the trail head, but at the same time, I thought to myself that she had asked a pertinent question, because the journey is never really over. But fortunately, sometimes, a savior appears, who takes the form of a yellow school bus.

The unknown possibilities of existence

As the omniscient and omnipotent Q told Captain Picard: "You just don't get it do you, Jean Luc? The trial never ends. We wanted to see if you had the ability to expand your mind and your horizons. And for one brief moment you did. For that one fraction of a second, you were open to options you had never considered. That is the exploration that awaits you. Not mapping stars and studying nebula, but charting the unknown possibilities of existence." ("Star Trek, The Next Generation," Episode 185).

Warriors saved for Saturday

I hope that one of the things that Haidyn has learned from her experience on the Hiawatha Trail is that we left our heavenly home so that we might chart for ourselves the unknown possibilities of existence. We have come "like gentle rain through darkened skies, with glory trailing from our feet as we go, and endless promise in our eyes. We are strangers from a realm of light, who have forgotten all - the memory of our former lives and the purpose of our call. And so, we must learn for ourselves why we're here, and who we really are." (Adapted from "Saturday's Warrior," lyrics by Doug Stewart).

The Infinite Atonement

Earlier, I mentioned the bus at the end of the trail, that was waiting to take us back to our car. Those who adapted the Hiawatha for cyclists provided a plan for all of its participants to follow, that included the convenience of transportation to take them back home. In all fairness, it was not a very pretty bus, and Haidyn may have been initially disappointed in its lack of amenities. As a matter of fact, the driver told us that there were a dozen or so buses, 4 or 5 of which were operable at any one time, the rest being held in reserve to be used for spare parts to keep at least a few running at any given time.

His tender mercies

As Haidyn waited with her parents and grandparents to board the bus, I thought about the thousands of workers who, over a hundred years ago, toiled to make the Route of the Hiawatha a reality. It was with my 9 year old granddaughter in mind that they designed, built, and maintained the roadbed. Long ago, it was envisioned and then constructed so that my grand-daughter might have a life-altering experience. When the rock was quarried, the trees felled, and the timbers sawn and hauled to the site, the grade surveyed, the rock blasted from the mountain sides, the ties and the track laid, and the spikes pounded in place, it was with Haidyn in mind. Their pre-emptive planning, construction, and preservation guaranteed that her experience in far-distant June 2015 would be a positive one.

It is not requisite
that we run faster
than we have strength

Even the grade had been surveyed with her in mind and to her benefit. Its gentle slope allowed her to set and maintain a comfortable pace, that she might not be tempted to cycle faster than she had strength and means. The constant grade spoke to her in a physical and tangible way, reminding her that the race is not to the swift, nor the battle to the strong, but to those who engage in a good cause, and who do many things of their own free will and choice.

O the greatness of His Plan

All that was necessary was for her to position herself in the zone, with her face oriented to the light, so that the shadows would always be behind her. Her obstacles would stimulate physical toughness, permit her to square off against psychological and emotional challenges, experience intellectual fortitude, and finally enjoy a spiritual synchronization that would allow her to more easily conquer adversity.

Our constant companion

As I watched her, I realized that what was responsible for her commendable performance was something that was more than physical. It was more than endorphins kicking in, and it was something greater than adrenaline that had given her a second wind. It was something metaphysical, as unconscious mechanisms guided her, and spiritual energy charged her with resolve. I know that if I had been able to put electrodes on her chest, I would have seen the screen of the EKG flashing with evidence that her heart was performing at an unusually high level of efficiency. She was not only burning fat, but also lethargy, indifference, mediocrity, and laziness. She was being infused with the spiritual element of an inner peace that surpasses understanding. After the Hiawatha, I am certain that she will never be the same. Nothing will rattle her cage.

Enter thou into my Rest

As we boarded the bus after the conclusion of our ride, we were hot and sweaty, tired and dusty, and thirsty and hungry. But that old bus was to Haidyn as a chauffeured limousine. I thought of something Boyd K. Packer said in a General Conference address, to the membership of the Church, many of whom must have felt as Haidyn did, hot and sweaty, tired and dusty, and thirsty and hungry from the exigencies of their mortal experiences.

He told the story of a World War II naval aviator, who left the security of his aircraft carrier to embark upon a dangerous mission. True to the predictions of his superior officers during the pre-flight briefing, he endured enemy anti-aircraft fire and engaged in potentially lethal dogfights.

His plane was hit numerous times by flack that tore away parts of his wings. His plexiglass canopy was shattered, and he could hardly see through blood-splattered goggles to navigate in bad weather back to his ship.

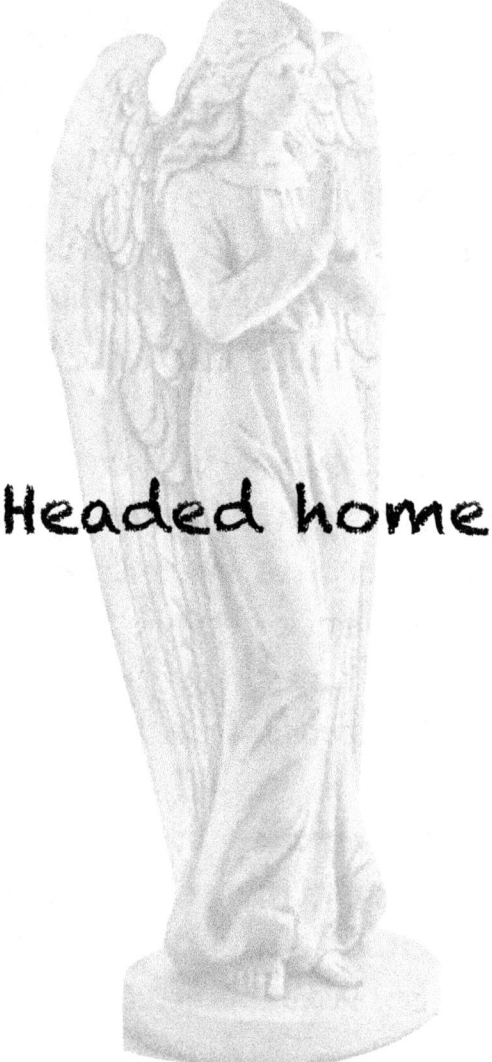

Headed home

As he came in for a landing on the pitching deck of the carrier, his controls were nearly useless, his descent too steep and his angle wrong. He was frantically waved off by the crewman on deck who was guiding him in, but he figured he had only one chance, and this was it. He would take it. With a sickening thump, as he pancaked his battered aircraft on the deck, the belly tank burst into flame, and the tail hook failed to engage the cables that would have safely jerked him to a halt. As he careened into the restraining net at the far end of the flight deck, what was left of his plane crumpled into twisted metal. A rescue crew in asbestos suits rushed to his aid, smothered the burning wreckage in fire-retardant foam, clamored up to the cockpit, cut through his harness, grabbed him by the shoulders, and dragged him out of danger. Doctors and nurses attended to his wounds even as he was carried to sick-bay. Due to their skill and attention, as well as to his unconquerable spirit, he made a remarkable and full recovery, and was awarded the Distinguished Flying Cross for uncommon valor.

This, Elder Packer suggested, is how most of us will return from our mortal mission to the presence of our Father.

May God so help each of us, as we draw closer to our rendezvous with destiny.

Keep pedaling

The hidden blessing that awaits those who successfully navigate their own personalized Hiawatha Trail is that they will find shelter from the vicissitudes and vagaries of life. Many years ago, Elder Vaughn Featherstone essentially told the Saints that they should stay on their bikes and keep pedaling! He said that the season of the world before us will be like no other in the history of mankind. It is clear that Satan has unleashed every evil, every scheme, every blatant, vile perversion ever known to man in any generation. Just as this is the dispensation of the fullness of times, so it is also the dispensation of the fullness of evil. We must seek shelter, he cautioned, and it is not to be found in the world. Wealth cannot provide it, law enforcement agencies cannot assure it, and membership alone in the Church cannot guarantee it.

As the evil night darkens upon this generation, we must create sanctuaries for light and safety, places that will be quiet, sacred havens where the storm cannot penetrate to harm us. There will be hosts of unseen sentinels watching over and guarding us, he assured us. Angels will attend us, and it will be as it was in the days of Elisha. Those that be with us will be more than they that be against us.

A darkening world

Before the Savior comes, there will be a period of time when even the elect of God may lose hope. The world will be so filled with evil that the righteous will only feel secure within the sacred walls of their homes and their temples that provide havens of peace.

Elder Featherstone declared: "I believe we may well have living on the earth now or very soon the boy who will be the prophet of the Church when the Savior comes." Those who will sit in the Quorum of Twelve Apostles are here, and so are those who will serve faithfully in the wards and stakes of Zion. These are the boys and girls who must be kept clean, sweet, and pure in a wicked world.

Follow the Covenant Path

Our garments will clothe us in a manner as protective as temple walls. Our covenants and the ordinances of the priesthood will fill us with faith as a living fire. In a day of desolating sickness, scorched earth, barren wastes, sickening plagues, disease, destruction, and death, we as a people will rest in the shade of trees and we will drink from cooling fountains. We will abide in places of refuge from the storm; we will mount up as upon eagles' wings; we will be lifted out of an insane and evil world. We will be as fair as the sun and clear as the moon.

Peace to last
a thousand years

The Savior will come and will honor His people. Those who are spared and prepared will know Him. They will cry out 'blessed be the name of He that cometh in the name of the Lord; thou art my God and I will bless thee; thou art my God and I will exalt thee.'

Our children will bow down at His feet and worship Him as the Lord of Lords and the King of Kings. They will bathe His feet with their tears, and He will weep and bless them for having suffered through the greatest trials ever known to man. His bowels will be filled with compassion and His heart will swell wide as eternity and He will love them. He will bring peace that will last a thousand years, and they will receive their reward to dwell with Him. Let us prepare our children with the faith to surmount every trial and every condition. (Adapted from an address delivered to the Utah South Stake, 4/1987).

A blueprint for survival in the Last Days

Haidyn is well on her way to enjoying that level of temporal and spiritual security and symmetry. The Hiawatha Trail, it seems, has provided her with more than a recreational opportunity. Like The Plan of Salvation itself, it has provided her with a blueprint for her survival in the Last Days.

Author's Note

One exciting
element that flows
from our resolve to
embrace adversity is the
constant stream of insight,
intuition, inspiration, and
revelation that cascades
down from above.

This
ensures that
we may walk along
illuminated pathways,
and use our faculties of
mind, intellect, and spirit to
more easily choose the better
part, although it may be more
difficult and we may face
daunting challenges
along the way.

As fire in
the sky, the air in
the theater of life will be
charged with an electricity that
represents the inevitable merger
of the universal encouragement
of the Light of Christ, with the
pointed and providential
guidance provided by
the Holy Ghost.

When these influences streak in tandem across the heavens, their trajectories will coalesce to trace a flaming trail that sparkles over a vast cosmic ocean of thought.

Over the ebb and
flow of its tide, the Spirit
will create an effectual bridge of
understanding between heaven and
earth, that is buttressed by the
cohesive influence of the
mighty foundation
of faith.

Then, the
perceived difficulty
of making the hard choice to
persevere in the face of obstacles,
and to endure in righteousness
to the end, will evaporate as
does the morning dew
in the noonday
sun.

Afterword

Latter-day prophets have consistently taught that those of the rising generation were valiant spirits in the tumultuous times of our pre-earth existence.

During the War
in Heaven, those who
stood with the Son of God
fought to preserve free will
as a foundation principle of
our Father's Plan of Salvation,
while those who rebelled with
Lucifer sought control of the
minds of men, through a
devious manipulation
of ideology.

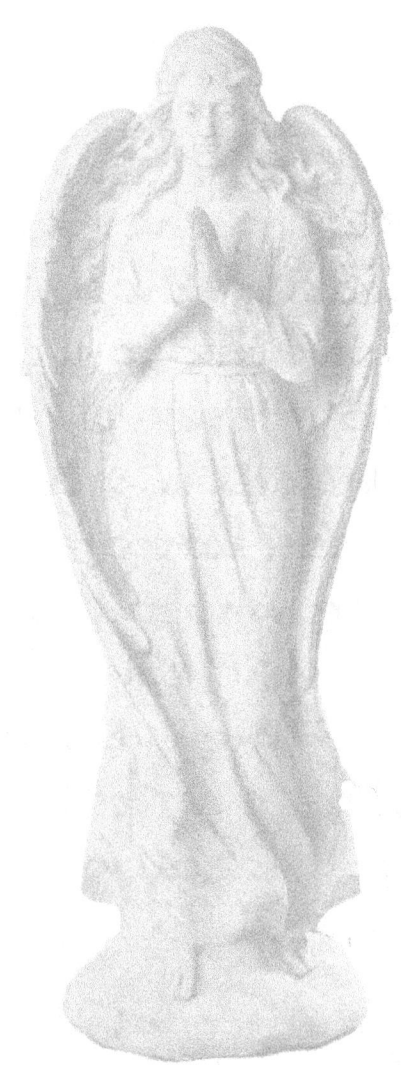

Those who were
zealous to defend their
right to freely express their
moral agency kept their first
estate, and were added upon.
They were blessed to come
to earth, that they might
fill the measure of
their creation.

During the pre-mortal conflict that pitted opposing philosophies against each other, the principle of free will prevailed, together with the natural consequences that are related to rebellion.

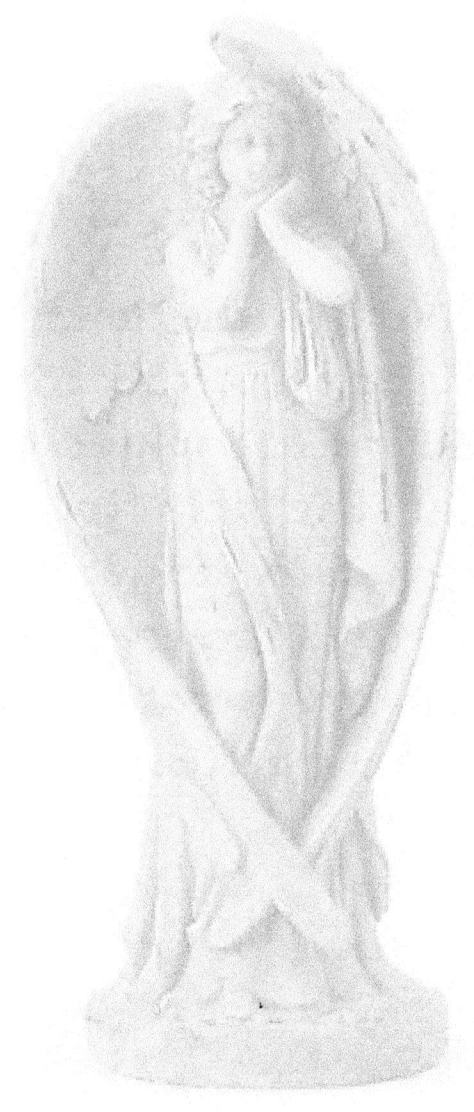

The
victorious spirit sons
and daughters of our Heavenly
Father have been blessed to engage
mortality with a passion that has been
ingrained within their nature by the
refiner's fire. They continue the
struggle, upon this temporal
stage, to safeguard their
God-given freedom to
choose their own
destiny.

Consequently, when those spirits who have come to earth to dwell in mortal clay sense that they are being controlled in any degree of unrighteousness, their innate tendency is to resist with the same fierce tenacity they exhibited in their pre-mortal life.

Therefore, in any scenario that involves the vigorous exercise of free will, if we wish to understand why others, and especially our youth, act as they do, it is helpful to view it from the perspective of the difficult journey they have made.

About The Author

Phil Hudson and his wife Jan have 7 children and over 25 grandchildren. They enjoy spending time with their family at their cabin nestled in the Selkirk Mountains, on the shore of Priest Lake, the crown jewel of North Idaho. Phil had a successful dental practice in Spokane, Washington for 43 years, before retiring in 2015. He has an eclectic mix of hobbies, and enjoys the out of doors. He always finds time, however, to record his thoughts on his laptop, and understands Isaac Asimov's response when he was asked: If you knew that you had only 10 minutes left to live, what would you do?" He answered: "I'd type faster."

Phil received the inspiration to write this book while he and Jan were serving as missionaries for The Church of Jesus Christ of Latter-day Saints, in the Kingdom of Tonga. While there, they celebrated their 50th wedding anniversary.

By The Author

Essays

    Volume One: Spray From The Ocean Of Thought
    Volume Two: Ripples On A Pond
    Volume Three: Serendipitous Meanderings
    Volume Four: Presents Of Mind
    Volume Five: Mental Floss
    Volume Six: Fitness Training For The Mind And Spirit

First Principles and Ordinances Series

    Faith - Our Hearts Are Changed
    Repentance - A Broken Heart and a Contrite Spirit
    Baptism - One Hundred And One Reasons Why We Are Baptized
    The Holy Ghost - That We Might Have His Spirit To Be With Us
    The Sacrament - This Do In Remembrance Of Me

Book of Mormon Commentary

    Volume One: Born In The Wilderness
    Volume Two: Voices From The Dust
    Volume Three: Journey To Cumorah

Doctrine & Covenants Commentary

    Volume One - Sections 1 - 34
    Volume Two - Sections 35 - 57

Minute Musings: Spontaneous Combustions of Thought

    Volume One
    Volume Two
    Volume Three

Calendars:

    As I Think About The Savior
    In His Own Words: Discovering William Tyndale
    Scriptural Symbols

Children & Youth

    Book of Mormon Hiking Song
    Happy Birthday
    Muddy, Muddy
    The Hiawatha Trail: An Allegory
    The Little Princess
    The Parable of The Pencil
    The Thirteen Articles of Faith

Doctrinal Themes

- Are Christians Mormon? Volume One
- Are Christians Mormon? Volume One
- Christmas is The Season When...
- Dentistry in The Scriptures
- Gratitude
- Hebrew Poetry
- Hiding in Plain Sight
- One Hundred Questions Answered by The Book of Mormon
- The Highways and Byways of Life
- The House of The Lord
- The Parable of The Pencil
- Without The Book of Mormon
- Writing on Metal Plates

A Thought For Each Day of the Year

- Faith
- Repentance
- Baptism
- The Holy Ghost
- The Sacrament
- The House of the Lord
- The Plan of Salvation
- The Atonement
- Revelation
- The Sabbath
- Life's Greatest Questions

Professional Publications

- Diode Laser Soft Tissue Surgery Volume One
- Diode Laser Soft Tissue Surgery Volume Two
- Diode Laser Soft Tissue Surgery Volume Three

These, and other titles, are available from online retailers.

Quid magis possum dicere?

www.ingramcontent.com/pod-product-compliance
Lightning Source LLC
Chambersburg PA
CBHW060506240426
43661CB00007B/935